LITVOICE 1

A LITERARY MAGAZINE

LITVOICE

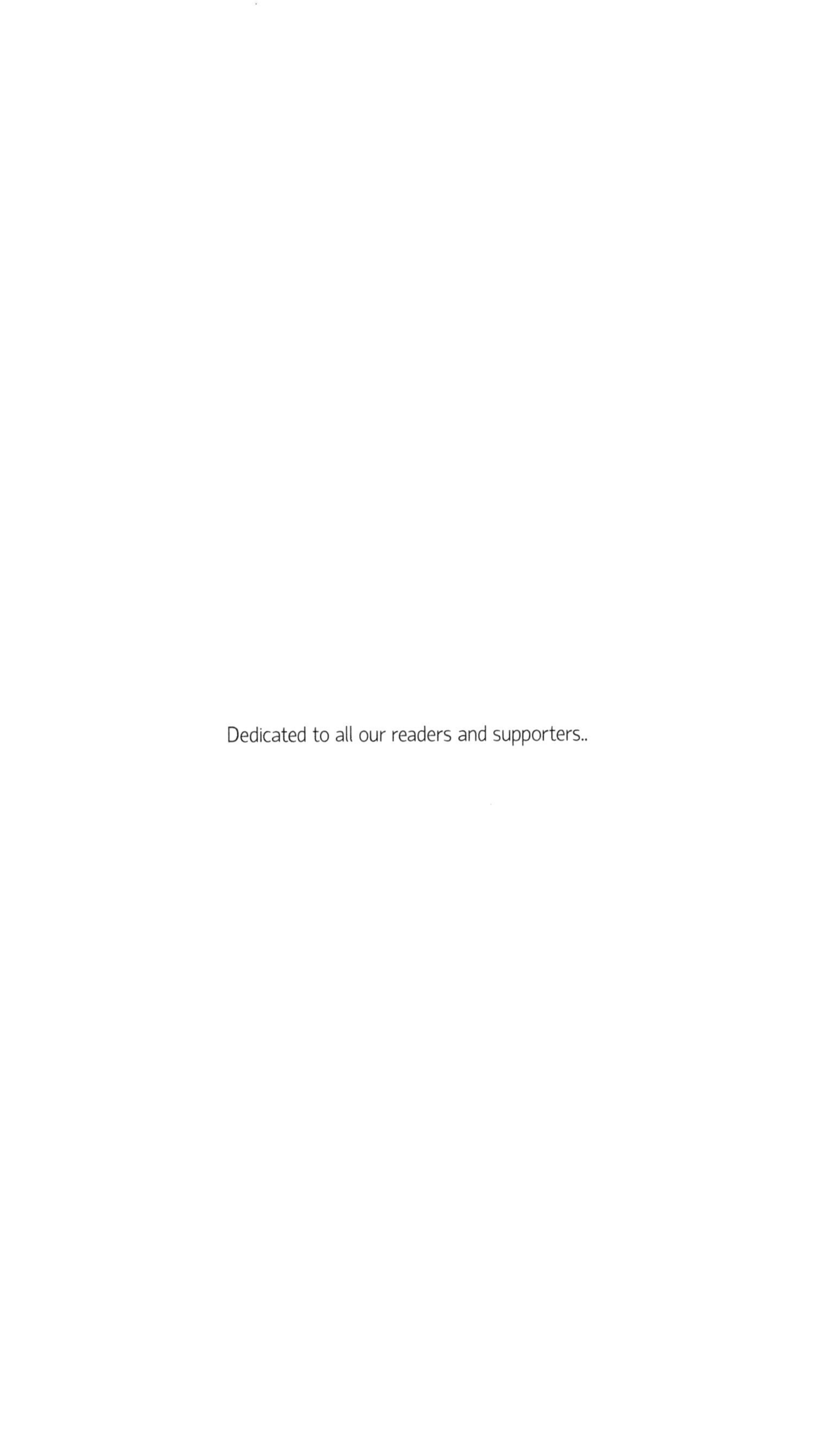

Dedicated to all our readers and supporters..

Contents

Foreword — vii

Preface — ix

Acknowledgements — xi

From The Editor's Desk — xiii

1. Cover Story - Dr. Sumit Goel — 1

2. Munmun Aidasani - An Author Of Change — 4

3. The Hunter's Moon Is October's Full Moon !! — 7

4. Open Letter To Brother - A Blessed Sister — 9

5. Covid 19 - Aisha — 11

6. Sangam : The Awakening - Book Review — 12

7. Best Summer Reads — 14

8. Author's Interview - Anupama Krishnan — 23

Foreword

" Literary voice " is a magazine of young writers. To express and to showcase their talent across the world.

Our own personal grouse with linguistic writing is that a great deal of it is far too technical for

(1) A general reader and

(2) A reader who doesn't want to fall asleep.

This is symptomatic of academic writing as a whole, of course; but that implies just how much of linguistics remains difficult to access if you don't have the requisite training and vocabulary (whose required level of familiarity sometimes boggles the mind).

I think a lot of what happens in linguistics is really, really good work that deserves to be recognized and championed for its worth and value to society, and used in multidisciplinary attempts to make the world a better place. Unfortunately, a lot of it can't reach the non-academically inclined person with big ideas because it's difficult to read and make sense of.

Preface

This is our 28th issue of " LitVoice " to reveal the voice of our unrevealed writers and poets...

Our aim is to showcase their unrevaled talent.... It's a passion. A love of words, and sentences, and subjectivities that make us all very much imperfect, and very much human, as we struggle to find words to express what we think and feel.

It remains only for me to thank you, my dear, cherished, highly sought-after reader. Thank you for reading this and supporting us, and I hope you come to love language as much as we do.

Welcome to "LitVoice". Let's reveal the world together...

Acknowledgements

LitVoice . We are Revealing Magazine for all ..now you all must think why this Name .. but " Literary Voice" was a better fit: it collocates nicely with a strong impact, this magazine is just an idea for giving us English Language majors something to do in our spare time. [There's another, even better reason, but I'll let you, the keen-eyed reader, figure it out].....hurray ..lets begin ...

From The Editor's Desk

Dear Reader:

In year 2018, in India, I started a little magazine devoted to fiction, poetry and literature. Firsty named "Literary Voice" then changed into "LitVoice" (Just a shorter version). LitVoice is India's leading bimonthly literary magazine. Since then we have published some of the best authors in and outside the country. Our generation grew up with the literature as a fact of life. India had many other magazine, but not a proper literature magazine to be called. India's literary magazine. To our minds, it is. It has launched our favorite writers. It has made a special claim for the quarterly as such, being both timely and lasting, free of the news of the day or the pressure to please a crowd. Most of all, the LitVoice has shown, repeatedly, that works of imagination can be as stylish and urgent as the flashiest feature reporting, and can do more to refocus our picture of the literature world.

Dedicated. Smart. Fearless. Strong. Eager to change the world. Willing to stay up late and awake before dawn to pursue their passion. Those are just a few words that describe our work at LitVoice Magazine. As my team and I pulled together the articles and writeups, that we think deserve to be shared.

When I read a literary magazine, I like to skip to the meaty insides. So, when it comes to the editor's note, I've always been a little suspicious of the genre. Editing, after all, is an invisible art. The work in this issue matters to me, and I hope it will matter to you. The package and the publicity matter to me too—those details might be part of what brought you here, to this note. My great hope is that you'll click out of here and go read this Issuewith great delight. It really needs no introduction, but it does need engaged readers through which to come alive. And hopefully when you're reading, you'll forget all about me and this note, which means I've done my job.

I think you'll be impressed.

Agrata Shanaya Shukla

Founder/ Chief Editor

CHAPTER ONE

Cover Story – DR. SUMIT GOEL

DR. SUMIT GOEL - M.D. (Hom) Gold Medalist
If your life were a book and you were the author, how would you want your story to go? That's the question that changed my life forever.

Dr. Sumit Goel with his book

"I feel privileged, honored and lucky, with the blessings of my parents to be in the noblest of all professions – A Teacher, A Doctor and an Author. -Dr. Sumit Goel"

Dr. Sumit Goel is a Doctor-Homoeopath by education and profession, a Teacher-Trainer by intention and a Motivator and Author by passion. The Teacher-Trainer Dr. Sumit Goel has been awarded with the "DYNAMIC PROFESSOR OF THE YEAR". Over a teaching span of more than 25 years, he has mentored, taught, trained thousands of medical students, who are today some of the leading names in healthcare sector in India and abroad. With a 99.33 excellent rating, he is one of the most sought-after teacher-trainer in the field. He believes that - "Education is what survives when what has been learned is forgotten." The Doctor-Homoeopath-Healer "The high and only mission of a physician is to restore the sick to health, to cure!" Dr. Sumit Goel belongs to an illustrious family of homoeopaths from Mumbai. His father, the famous Late Dr. Sunil Kumar Goel was one of the seniormost homoeopaths from western

India. Dr. Sumit has been practising now for more than 25 years. He has provided a healing touch to innumerable patients over the years with his healing smile, motivational words and the white pill. He amalgamates the latest approaches in health management and life transformation technology to achieve the highest ideal of healthy living. He actively pursues telemedicine so as to reach to patients across the globe and integrates technology in treatment. He has been awarded with "YOUNG ACHIEVER'S AWARD" for "Great contribution to the field of Homoeopathy".

The Author

Dr. Sumit Goel has been one of the youngest authors in the field of medical text. At the young age of 29, his first medical book was instantly recognised as the standard text for medical students in India and abroad. Having penned many medical books, he has been awarded the BEST AUTHOR, in the field of medical literature.

The Motivational Author

"I WANNA GROW UP ONCE AGAIN" is one of the finest works by an Indian Author in the genre of motivational self-help self-empowerment transformational books. The book has an Introduction by respected Anupam Kher. The book has been appreciated and well received by luminaries and readers alike. He is the recipient of "BEST MOTIVATIONAL AUTHOR" and is recipient of "HIGH FLYERS 50 GLOBAL INDIANS AWARD along with many other literary awards for his work. The book – I WANNA GROW UP ... ONCE AGAIN – Change the Perception, Break the Pattern is an inward journey into how we have lived our life, till now ... and how we choose to live from now!

It is about the journey of transformation, of the awareness and acceptance of our perceptions and patterns and the action of changing the perception and breaking the pattern. As we grow up, we try to understand life, ourselves and the world around us. These understandings are our Perceptions. Our perception becomes a reality for us. We start to live with certain perceptions about our self. We feel we are alone. We feel nobody seems to understand us. We feel we are not good enough. We think ourselves a failure. Our Perceptions lead to our Patterns of behaviour. These patterns become repetitive. We seem to perceive and react in the same pattern again and again. And most of the times, these patterns of behavior are something that we find difficult to break. We find ourselves caught in loops in life. Stories are different, situations are different, our patterns remain the same.

And a time comes in all our lives, when we tell ourselves – I wanna grow up ... once again. "When we shift our perception, our experience changes." There is no greater power in the universe than thought. What is mind, nothing but thoughts. The moment we have the awareness, acknowledgement and acceptance of this, starts the process of "Change the Perception, Break the Pattern". Transformation does not lie in changing the past or controlling our environment. It lies within.

What happens to us is not important. What happens in us is important. Transformation is not an event. It is a journey. It is not a specific moment in our life. It is a continuous process of empowered living. This journey of transformation traverses the three steps of Awareness, Acceptance and Action!

The book tries to connect us to certain deeper parts of us with thought provoking issues like Why we don't do what we want to do! Why do we hold on, why do we not let go!

We all make efforts, but how do we handle setbacks and burnouts! How to identify and manage our triggers! How to change our perceptions and break our patterns!

Dr. Sumit Goel can be connected at sumitgoel@yahoo.com or visit him at www.drsumitgoel.com

When you go into the space of nothingness, everything becomes known!

CHAPTER TWO

Munmun Aidasani - An Author of change

Munmun Aidasani, author of "Never the same"

Munmun aidasani, was born to the loving parents of city of lakes - Bhopal (India) and spent childhood with an inspiration and ambition to grow and be successful in every field she steps in. This aspiration to excel has led her to give an inordinate amount of her youth nosing through books of finance and headed towards receiving undergraduate degrees and Masters in Finance, and went on to work in a corporate job while pursuing a career in finance and holds the Charter as a Financial Analyst with utter pride.

This personal and academic growth she proudly credits to her loving and supporting husband and family as she procured the degree after getting married to the dashing and renowned businessman of Dubai (U.A.E). She started her writing journey as a blogger, then and there her writing career flourished. The Reader Street is her platform, where she is documenting her thoughts, experiences and learnings for readers to quench their thirst of reading and digest the chief matter of numerous articles.

Apart from this she has consistently contributed her work in various anthologies. She is aspiring to become a top-notch writer and engross the readers through her words, as she believes that words have the power to heal the minds. Herself being prolific thinker and huge admirer of sayings and belief of "Gaur Gopal Das" as she follows his approach towards life "Neither are born winners nor are we born losers. We are born choosers. We can all choose. We all have choices to make." She asserts that It's any writer's greatest fear: facing the blank page with no ideas to get started. Multi genre writing can be a challenge, but it can also be a way to fulfill the different parts of your creative needs, which can be definitely channeled into different ways of telling stories. There are different parts of your personality that make you up which cannot be reconciled into one single voice all the time. If you want to grab the attention of your readers, you have to find high concept ideas for your books. Though author is often remembered for one genre in particular but she simply concentrate on making the work that is interesting and unique as by putting content out there, as you're essentially asking readers to borrow their time for what you've written. So the idea of value comes in when your readers have something to gain from it, after all when people read, they conjure the images and feelings from their own experience of life, not yours. She claims that - It is imperative that you read in the genres you intend to write in- not only read, but absolutely fall in love with books, characters, paragraphs, dialogue, styles or sound of the

language within that genre. She follow this simple rule: whatever you love reading is what you should be writing, it's like she doesn't want to limit herself to one genre. Yes she always has certain books on her shelf that she couldn't connect like it doesn't work for her but she keep few volumes around even though she doesn't like.

Writing in multiple genres has a steep learning curve, and you may face enormous amounts of rejection, which can bring on crippling self-doubt, but for her lack of confidence does not mean a lack of talent. She adds,

Writing articles and stories is an excellent way to develop your voice. Learn to embrace the many versions of yourself. Sometimes you don't enjoy writing, but still to write regularly gives you a deep satisfaction and helps you to stop collapsing emotionally from within.

She is an Author, an Optimist, a Poetess, a Swash-buckling action-adventure Romantic Fiction Novelist and a Motivational Writer. She is trying to be a major voice in the world of personal development and spiritual wisdom. She is using her positive influence to spread good vibes only through her books and articles so that people can unlock their full potential and demonstrate greatness in all areas of their life.

"NEVER THE SAME- THE CONVENTIONAL TALES OF UNCONVENTIONAL MOMS", is beautifully weaved by her based on the facts of motherhood. There is a joy in hearing wisdom, tales that your heart takes and translates into your life, your language, your being. Some of her observations are wildly funny, others bittersweet, but above all a comfort to know that there are mothers out there in the same boat and you are not alone in both good and bad experiences. If you are one of those who closely follows her then surely she has given you another reason to keep your passion alive. She is working on various other books and novella which will keep you hooked up with its brevity and inimitable style.

She believes we can't help everyone but everyone can help someone. Going far beyond the call of duty, doing more than others expect is what excellence is all about. For her success and growth can only be measured by how much you help others because to serve is beautiful but the only thing it should be done with joy and a whole heart and a free mind. The sole meaning of her life is to "Serve Humanity", as kindness is the only key to transform someone's dark moment with a blaze of light. She is the Founder of Adhikaar Organization (NGO), team which is made up of people from different walks of life, from different families and backgrounds. They are passionate about turning the everyday moments of the less privileged and needy people into memories and celebrating the beautiful relationship with them and brighten their life with all the bright hues of life.

Her wit, generosity of spirit, love for her family is vivid and compelling. Anyone who has listened to her words will already know that she's a mesmerizing inspirer. Significant for the perspective that rich and famous or not, in the end it's our values that define us.

CHAPTER THREE

The Hunter's Moon Is October's Full Moon !!

October's Full Moon is the Hunter's Moon. It is also called Travel Moon, Dying Grass Moon, and sometimes Blood Moon or Sanguine Moon.

Deer are hunted in the month of October.

When are the Full Moons this year?

Harvest Moon Some Years

Every three years, the October Full Moon is also the Harvest Moon. This particular name is given to the Full Moon which is closest to the September equinox, which is the start of fall in astronomy.

However, the astronomical seasons do not match up with the lunar month. Therefore, the month the Harvest Moon occurs in, varies. Most years, it is in September. However, every three years, it is in the month of October.

Where Do Full Moon Names Come From?

In ancient times, it was common to track the changing seasons by following the lunar month rather than the solar year, which the 12 months in our modern calendar are based on.

For millennia, people across Europe, as well as Native American tribes, named the months after features they associated with the Northern Hemisphere seasons, and many of these names are very similar or identical.

Today, we use many of these ancient month names as Full Moon names. A common explanation is that Colonial Americans adopted many of the Native American names and incorporated them into the modern calendar.

However, it seems that it is a combination of Native American, Anglo-Saxon, and Germanic month names which gave birth to the names commonly used for the Full Moon today.

Some years have 13 Full Moons, which makes one of them a Blue Moon, as it doesn't quite fit in with the traditional Full Moon naming system. However, this is not the only definition of a Blue Moon.

Hunter's Moon or Blood Moon

Hunter's moon is mentioned in several sources as the Anglo-Saxon name for the Full Moon of October. This is the month when the game is fattened, and it is time to start preparing for the coming winter. Traditionally, this included hunting, slaughtering and preserving meats for use in the coming winter months.

Other names are Travel Moon and Dying Grass Moon. Some also called it Blood Moon or Sanguine Moon, which also refers to the hunting season. However, this name should not be confused with the term Blood Moon to describe a Total Lunar Eclipse.

CHAPTER FOUR

Open letter to brother – A Blessed sister

Dear bro,

The most anticipated day of the year have come again but the tragedy of this day is that, unlike all the years that we have spent this day together, this year we are so far apart. It feels off-kilter and sad all at the same time. I wish we had been together this Rakhi as well, doing all our conventional leg pulling and teasing the way we used to.

I am blessed to have a brother like you and the words won't justify the amount of respect and love I have for you. As mother fondly recalls the time when I first arrived, you were scared to hold me, you were scared that this miniature baby would crumble if you touch her so much and I may somehow vanish. You were fascinated by my small hands and spend counting each finger twice a day. A four-year-old boy got a little toy to play with and he was ecstatic. This baby grew up to be your partner-in-crime, playmate, little nuisance and sometimes a total pain in the ass.

You made me what I am today. You made me strong, wild, independent and sassy. We have made the plethora of memories together and played countless of made up games throughout the day and night. If I never had your calming presence, I would have been a sad case of a classic spoilt brat but you grounded me.

We shared our own secret world of imaginary pirates, you were Peter Pan and I was one of the lost boys, fighting captain Hook, climbing imaginary mountains, going on epic quests for lost treasures. It was just you, me and our backyard. How can I forget all the senseless things we tried and got trashed within the inch of our life?

This day all the memories are replaying through my brain on an endless loop. I wish I can somehow transcend space and time and reach you to tie that one sacred thread and not break the one ritual that we have been doing together since we were in diapers. As a kid, we did this to satisfy our mother and competed over who has better rakhi. I was jealous of the shiny diamonds and pretty designs that winked at me from your wrist. So, I would cry and you would always remove the shiniest rakhi from your wrist and tie it on mine. As we grew older, it was not a competition anymore but a deep sense of sentimentality and emotions whenever I tied it on your wrist. It was renewal of the promise that we shared and a ritual that promised so much without uttering a single word. I will terribly miss this ritual because it signifies that we have been through so much. We have grown up together with our grandmother's stories whispering magical realms into our ears, weaving dream worlds distant and untouched and the echoes of gods mighty and strong. It shows that we have shared bruises, tears and all the mighty adventures that makes the childhood most beautiful phase ever.

So, even though we are far apart, our heart is still together. It lies in the distant fields of unripe maize where we played hide and seek, it still beats in the silent echoes of the laughter that we shared while rolling down the hills and it would always find it's peace at the end of the day in the childish antics buried deep in our memories. Photographs can only capture frozen memories but this heart replays those memories and brings it to life. I'll always cherish these memories in my heart. Forever.

Happy Rakshabandhan Bhai.

Yours Lovingly,

A Sister that still trails behind you

CHAPTER FIVE

Covid 19 – Aisha

Let's talk about this pandemic - very serious news that came into the world.

What was our life like before all this?

You have wondered how drastically our thinking changed after the first rumour; for many, it is just one rumour more, for others, it is the fall of something grave.

The things we did, the places we went, without asking ourselves what will happen tomorrow.

Sometimes there is no explanation for why things happen. We know why, but under such circumstances, the human being is not programmed to obey 100%.

It's the law of life, and it's here we break the chain. Above all, I see sadness, nostalgia, madness everywhere; but nevertheless I see a united Mexico because there are more people who do good than those who do evil, more people who do their part for society.

What worries me most is not going out anymore, not seeing my loved ones, and taking hold of the life I used to have - even though sometimes I didn't value it as I should have.

Despite the circumstances, I'm still standing. I do what I like from home, whether it is the same experience or not.

Even though I miss going out to have fun, I know that the day will come when they will tell us the news that we will all be free,

the day when we will all carry with us a great lesson:

That time is now, today. Let's take action, let's save one more life, even if we don't know them. We will join forces so that all this comes to pass, we will come out of this problem, and we will rise up to be better, because we are people with aspirations, goals, dreams, all together for the world"

CHAPTER SIX

Sangam : The Awakening – Book Review

"Sangam: The Awakening" is a beautiful crafted, epic tale of a Kingdom which is in turmoil due to an impending prophecy. A book on politics, mystery with a sprinkle of magic, Sangam the Awakening is Indian historical fiction at its best. Set in the kingdom of Devaprastha with an ailing king and a devoted chief minister. The story takes a mysterious turn when a planned assassination with ties to the inner members of the king's ministers, shows that the kingdom is under threat. Political instability, outer enemies and an age old prophecy, this book is a journey for the senses.

The story has the influence of history fiction mixed with suspense and thriller. It has a pretty unique plot as the book focuses on the scenario going in a fictional kingdom. While the commander of the kingdom comes across two kids, a pair of twins who have a mysterious link to themselves. But it is only realised after years, when the kingdom is falling down. What is teh significance of these two mysterious kids? Are they a blessing or curse for the kingdom?

The story begins with the murder of innocent people which turn out to be a curse for the kingdom. It has called upon the downfall of the kingdom. The story is of a kingdom that faces doom in the face of a deadly prophecy. It is about humans wielding secret powers, people discovering their unexpected ancestry and about decisions that can put the fate of the kingdom in question.

The author Tejaswini Sundar's intellect in stitching the various segments of the story is commendable. Consequently, her book never ceases to enchant and thrill the readers. With a lot happening in each and every corner of the story, with the sequences packed with action, the book becomes a grand affair to witness. Like every other historical fiction, Tejaswini has tried to build her plot in a layered manner. She keeps true to a primary plot, with certain sub-plots paving the way to more exciting storytelling. Her characters are diverse and numerous, and they all have roles to play in the various plots.

The author has taken enough time to build the world of the book thus its a well paced plot with slow descriptions sometimes. There are numerous characters yet each character development has been presented well.

"Sangam The Awakening" is not only a mind-blowing creation but also a very engrossing story indeed.

For all the Fantasy lovers... grab this masterpiece now !!

CHAPTER SEVEN

Best Summer Reads

1. Book Name: Canvas Of Feelings by Prateek Singh

Genre: Poetry

Format: Paperback/Kindle

MRP: 150 INR

Available at: Available at: My Secret Bookshelf Online Store, Amazon, Flipkart, Notion Press Online Store.Blurb: The Canvas of Feelings is a poetry book in which unspoken, unheard, and suppressed emotions are inked which the Broken Souls try to utter but fail to mumble. The book follows a journey of an individual who is going through varied emotions in his life; From Heart-Break to Love; From Love to being Lost. As the person rides through varied waves of emotion he found his best friend a PEN.

From where he started his journey to pour the mumbles, the inner screams, the saddened scenic view around him on the Canvas. Come along and follow his journey from being broken to finding his voice and getting lost in the way of finding the truth.

2. Meghna by Devika Das
Genre:Hindi Contemporary Fiction
Format: Paperback/ Kindle
MRP:120 INR
Available at: Amazon, Flipkart, Blue Rose Publishers Online Store, Barnes Noble.
Blurb: Acting comes under the umbrella of performing arts. The actors perform on stage/cinema to entertain the public, but the audience is unaware of their real life experiences. They idolize the actors and forget that they too have a human side. An actor's life may be diametrically opposite to

the character played in a play/film. Reel life vs real life. This story exhibits the emotional aspects of the real-life of an award-winning theatre artist, Meghna Sahay, through a retrospective narrative. The poems mentioned in this story are original works of the author.

3. Book Name: Autumn: The Mosaic of All by Roobal Gupta
Genre: Young Adult Fiction
Format: Paperback/Kindle
MRP: 150 INR
Available at: Amazon
Blurb: Has a nightmare ever kept you wide awake, all night?
Scaring you to death all day, every day threatening to reveal your past? Have you ever felt the shadow of terrible emptiness following you all around? "Stumbling. Broken. Weird. Confused. Introvert." Do any of these define even the smallest part of you?
Zoya is a confused girl who is dealing with similar weird thoughts, swirling in her mind like a whirlwind. She has found her little recluse in Kabir, her amazing best friend. He is one happy-go-lucky guy who, unknowingly, keeps her alive and happy with his innocence and mirth. But her life

changes after Aarav walks into it and sweeps her off her feet with his boyish charm and positive attitude. Walk

along with these amazing characters along their joyful journey of Ad self-discovery and self-worth.

How difficult it is to let go off your past and to what extent would your friends go to save you from it?

"Autumn: The Mosaic of All" is a powerful and touching story of friendship, betrayal, strength and above all love and self-belief.

4. Book Name: Love Try Angle by Manali Desai
Genre: Romance Comedy
Format: Kindle(Paperback releasing in June)
MRP: 69 INR
Available at: Amazon
Blurb: Ayesha has just moved to the 'City of Dreams' with her parents. She befriends the charming Viren, who helps her find her footing in Mumbai. Though she is slowly adjusting to her new life, what Ayesha is most excited about is pursuing B.A. (Hons.) Political Science from a reputed college. Things don't go as smoothly as she had thought though. Because Abhi, her senior, seems hell-bent on making her life on the campus difficult from day one. Just when things seem settled, Viren joins the college as an Ad-Hoc

lecturer. Is there more to Ayesha's friendship with Viren, and her frenemity with Abhi? It seems there's a love triangle blooming around the corner or will it be a Love (Try) Angle? Because Ayesha is not sure if it's love at all.

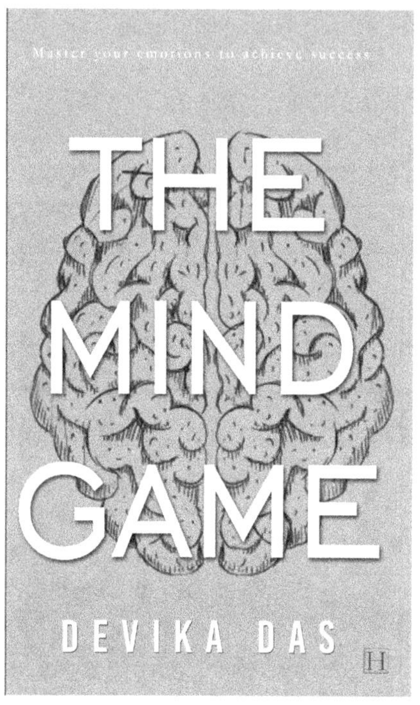

5. Book Name: The Mind Game by Devika Das
Nonfiction self help
   Format: Paperback
MRP: 205 INR
Available at: Amazon , Flipkart
Blurb: Happiness, stress, ecstasy or depression, it s all a mind game. As long as our mind is under our control, everything else is. That s what The Mind Game is all about. It is not an average self-help book that preaches life-enhancing methodologies based on complex science or long philosophical verses. The book is genius lies in its simplicity. It offers quick, actionable and instantly applicable tips that will help readers lead better lives, instantly.

6. Book Name: Somehow I Missed It by Poorvaja Pooja Sharma
Genre: Crime Fiction
Format: Paperback/Kindle
MRP: 399 INR
Available at: Amazon
Blurb: If we get a gut feeling that something isn't right about a person or situation, should we trust it or ignore it? You will obviously say Trust it. But I ignored it with my strong will power. Do I regret it? Not at all. In fact I am proud of it. But why and how? I did experience a crime, which I have jotted down in this novel "Somehow I missed it". I found a friend. This friend is a murderer serving life imprisonment. Please read to find out why I am proud of my dear Murderer friend. A murderer has a heart and is also a human being and he is not a Monster. This crime novel has everything from real paranormal incidents to the philosophy of life that I discovered.

7. Book Name: Speaking From The Autumn Of My Life by Sarbajit Chowdhury

Genre: Poetry

Format: Paperback

MRP: 98 INR

Available at: Amazon, Flipkart, Shopclues, Blue Rose Publishers Online Store

Blurb: This book contains poems that deal with various themes such as love, lust, the illusion of beauty, affection, trust, patriotism, child abuse, etc. We, as human beings, do play a plethora of roles in our lives, and we often dive deep into our roles. The essence of each relationship, emotions, and role is important. Being an extremely emotional child, I had always given priority to my emotions but failed to express them. Much later in life, I started expressing myself through poems. Each word written in this book has its own essence and importance. I believe to the core that emotions are the essence of one's existence, and they

are best expressed through words. Penning down my feelings through words was difficult, and was an emotional process. The words in this book reflect my hard work. They are an ode to my true feelings and real-life experiences. I hope you will like the poems and relate to them at some point of time.

8. Book Name: Mrs Basu's Uncensored Familism by Chirasree Bose
Genre: Humour
Format: Paperback/Kindle
MRP: 199 INR
Available at: Amazon, Flipkart, Google Books
Blurb: Mrs. Arpita base, the only daughter-in-law of base family, is here to tell you a story that will leave your stomach hurting with chuckles and laughter. A chudail to her prim mother-in-law, inexistent to the devil father-in-law, a damped down bomb to her once best friend naveena and well, nothing whatsoever to her own husband. Akash, the 23-year-old finds herself questioning the very concept of familism as her six months of tumultuous married life is hit with unanswerable questions sprouting every now and then in
her head. Speaking of head, what do you think is its importance in Mrs. Basu's life? Oh boy, you're in for a surprise! Because the quirks of their tongue-in-cheek relationship is bound to make you split your sides.

However, in a split second Mrs. Basu's life goes kaput as her dark past comes knocking at the door. While
she struggles to keep it at Bay, her husband leaves her side with no promise of coming back ever.Is it a mere coincidence that her past holds a connection to the disappearance of her husband? Or, is it what Mrs. Basu deserves for all she did in the past? This chapter of her life will unravel the mysteries of the present, all the knots of the past and the road to the future. Of course, in the most hilarious way possible.

CHAPTER EIGHT

Author's Interview – Anupama Krishnan

Author Anupama Krishnan

Q1. Tell us a bit about yourself.
I am Anupama Krishnan-" A bit of life for poetry, a bit of poetry for life". A product manager by
profession and a poet by passion, I am an avid reader with vivid imagination. A keen observer of life, I
am often overwhelmed by thoughts and raw emotions. What began as jotting down of bits and pieces of

thought, eventually shaped into poems and prose and into books with time.

Q2. How did publishing your first book change your process of writing?
I did not write with the aim to publish. I wrote because I always felt life was fleeting and there are so
many thoughts and emotions that are lost in daily living. Sometimes it is in these fleeting thoughts and
moments that we have clarity and original thoughts, but they are often washed down by time. My
writing process has always been an attempt to capture these moments that is forever forgotten in
history, and publishing these just happened with time.
The process of writing remains the same, although because of publishing I have been able to reach a
wider audience. Kids from the age of 10yo to 75 yo adults have written to me after reading the book and
it is definitely a feeling of gratitude.

Q3. If you could tell your younger writing self, anything, and what would it be?
Read a lot of books. Read different genres and also authors from various countries. Read non
conventional books, develop your voice. The most important aspect for any writer is to develop your
voice. Read and write a lot without any inhibition so that you can identify your voice. Do not fear what
people will think of you. Do not feel judged, do not lose your heart if others don't understand. Your
writing is your personal journey and it will unfold the way it has to be. Do not force yourself to fit in.

Q4. What does literary success look like to you?
There are various ways to measure success of a book, number of sales, awards, amazon review etc. But
to me a book is successful if it can stand the test of time, if it connects to various people from different
age groups, ethnicity, upbringing and socio economic background. If the book can appeal to human

heart and mind and leave them with some after thoughts. If the book can have a life of its own, outside

the writer, then the book is a warrior, a winner and that's what literary success means to me.

Q5. Does your family support your career as a writer?
I am work in IT as product manager, my job pays my bills. Writing is my way of expressing myself. I had

started writing at the age of 13, although it was not shared with anyone for a very long time. My

husband has been a great support with my book launch. I do not look at writing as my career. I am not

sure if I want to pursue writing as a full time carrier and I am sure if I do, I will have full support of my

family.

Q6. What one thing would you give up to become a better writer?
   I would give up my idea of 'anupama as a writer' to be a better writer. As we write we realize that we

have conflicting thoughts. For eg sometimes we write about love as the ultimate meaning to life and

other times as root cause of all evil. If we define ourselves to be an ambassador of a particular thought,

then we lose out on every other thought that we pass through. In my mind it is important to be tag free

so that we can truly and sincerely express the diversities of human mind.

Q7. Who's your Inspiration in the literary field?
I look up to many writers, Toni Morrison, Virgina Woolf, Jhumpa Lahri, Ayn Rand etc are some woman

writers who have influenced me greatly. Among men I am forever grateful to Herman Hesse, Fernando

Pessoa, Camus, Gabriel Gracia Marcus and many more. I guess its difficult to pick a name because as we

evolve, we discover writers and our influences also keep changing.

Q8. What kind of research do you do, and how long do you spend researching before beginning a book?

Most of my research happens after the book is written and it is in the form of beta reading to find that

space, the gaps between the book that you have in mind vs the book that people can connect to and

understand. I mean it's great to write a book just by your ideas, but somewhere we need to be sure that

there is an audience for it. It's mostly through the process of beta reading that I evolve the book to meet

the expectations of market.

Q9. What's the turning point of your life when you realize you want to be an author?

I always knew I am a writer for life. Publishing and becoming an author was a natural progression. I write to make sense of my life and my existence. Writing is my way of expressing myself, to some people its dance, to others cooking etc. But we all have a way of expressing ourselves, and we always know that in our heart, may be the process of realizing it is gradual for some and sudden for others. I knew writing was my way since my teenage.

Q10. How long on average does it take you to write a book?

3 months.

Q11. What are your favorite literary books?

Tough one, this is a just a sample

? Beloved- Toni Morrison

? Interpreter of Maladies – Jumpha Lehri

? Alice in Wonderland – Lewis Carol

? One hundred years of solitude : Gabriel Gracia Marquez

? Little Price : Antoine De Saint

I can't do this.. the list is too long.

Q12. Why have you selected to write in this genre?

I write poetry and prose mostly because It comes naturally to me and also because it easily fits into my

otherwise hectic work schedule. I can think and form ideas while I am driving or when I am having food

and write it out later, in 30 mins. There is more time and research required for fiction. I think I have parked it for later when I have more time or when a story comes to me, whichever happens first.

Q13. Do you hide any secrets in your books that only a few people will find?
Oh yeah, I guess people write because we live a masked life, hiding our true self somewhere behind. We
play the roles suited for the society and culture while knowing that we are beyond our roles. I don't
think we hide secrets as such, but yes throughout time artists have used art to express freely and
differently from their daily lives. I think art exist because there is always some unexpressed, unresolved
emotion within.
Q14. Do you view writing as a kind of spiritual practice?
Writing or any art to me is a spiritual practice of holding on and letting go.

Q15. What's the best way to market your books?
I think there are many ways available nowadays, blogs, paid campaigns, podcasts. You have to find the
one that works best for you, a channel where your target audience is present.

www.ingramcontent.com/pod-product-compliance
Lightning Source LLC
Chambersburg PA
CBHW061646130726
47996CB00003B/1481